BRILLIANCE™

UNCOMMON VOICES FROM UNCOMMON WOMEN™

COMPILED BY
DAN ZADRA WITH SUSAN CARLSON

DESIGNED BY
KOBI YAMADA AND STEVE POTTER

COM·PEN´·DI·UM™
INCORPORATED

PUBLISHING & COMMUNICATIONS

ACKNOWLEDGEMENTS

The author of the Brilliance™ collection wishes to express his sincere appreciation to Seattle writer, lecturer and business consultant Susan Carlson whose seminars and workshops are widely acclaimed. Susan's seminar brochure describes her simply as "a pebble kicker for women." Her remarkable track record as a consultant for some of America's most dynamic young companies proves she also moves mountains.

WITH SPECIAL THANKS TO

John Applegate, Gerry Baird, Justi Baumgardt, Neil Beaton, Hal Belmont, Beth Bingham, Doug Cruickshank, Jim Darragh, Josie and Rob Estes, Jennifer Hurwitz, Dick Kamm, Beth Keane, Liam Lavery, Connie McMartin, Teri O'Brien, Janet Potter & Family, Diane Roger, Robert & Val Yamada, Tote Yamada, Anne Zadra, Augie & Rosie Zadra and August & Arline Zadra.

CREDITS

Compiled by Dan Zadra with Susan Carlson

Designed by Kobi Yamada and Steve Potter

ISBN: 0-9640178-0-6

Printed in Hong Kong

Thoughts
To Inspire
&
Celebrate
Your Achievements™

B R I L L I A N C E

Brilliance may be difficult to describe, but we all know it when we see it. It's a bright idea, a daring decision, an ingenious insight, a soaring aspiration, or a wise and compassionate action.

"Brilliance is one part talent, two parts wisdom and three parts passion," wrote Pulitzer Prize winning novelist Margaret Mitchell. "Whenever you encounter it in your midst, celebrate it, encourage it, be happy for it."

This little book is one way of doing just that. It's a treasury of wise and wonderful quotations–a celebration of life, love and work–from some of the most creative and accomplished women of our times.

BRILLIANCE

"Brilliance" is not so much a book about women as it is a book about life through a woman's eyes. It celebrates and encourages some of the best parts of the human spirit–our everyday cares, concerns and commitments, our dreams, hopes and plans, our mistakes, setbacks and triumphs.

We hope we have created a book that both men and women will savor, treasure and keep. We think you'll soon discover, however, that the real joy and satisfaction comes from giving it away. Look around. Someone in your midst is brilliant. Celebrate them. Encourage them. Be happy for them.

The future belongs to those who believe in the beauty of their dreams.

–Eleanor Roosevelt

Reality is something you rise above.

–Liza Minnelli

*I might have been born
in a hovel, but I was determined to travel
with the wind and the stars.*

–Jacqueline Cochran

Longing performs all things.

–Mary Renault

*We know not where our dreams
will take us, but we can probably see quite clearly
where we'll go without them.*

—Marilyn Grey

❧

When nothing is sure, everything is possible.

—Margaret Drabble

❧

*Dreams come a size
too big so that we can grow into them.*

—Josie Bisset

BRILLIANCE

*If one is lucky,
a solitary fantasy can totally transform
one million realities.*

—Maya Angelou

❧

*We couldn't conceive
of a miracle if none had ever happened.*

—Libbie Fudim

❧

*Reach high, for stars
lie hidden in your soul. Dream deep,
for every dream precedes the goal.*

—Pamela Starr

If I had influence with the good fairy,
I would ask that her gift to each child be a sense
of wonder so indestructible that it would
last throughout life.

–Rachel Carson

❧

Hope is the thing
with feathers that perches in the soul,
and sings the tune without the words,
and never stops at all.

–Emily Dickinson

*Begin doing what you want
to do now. We are not living in eternity.
We have only this moment, sparkling like a star in
our hand—and melting like a snowflake.*

–Marie Beynon Ray

❧

*If it's a good idea,
go ahead and do it. It is much easier to
apologize than it is to get permission.*

–Admiral Grace Murray Hopper

BRILLIANCE

*It takes as much
energy to wish as it does to plan.*

–Eleanor Roosevelt

❧

*When people
keep telling you that you can't do a thing,
you kind of like to try it.*

–Margaret Chase Smith

❧

Action is the antidote to despair.

–Joan Baez

*You can't wring
your hands and roll up your sleeves
at the same time.*

–Michele Brown

❧

*What the hell–
you might be right, you might be wrong...
but don't just avoid.*

–Katharine Hepburn

❧

*You may be disappointed
if you fail, but you are doomed
if you don't try.*

–Beverly Sills

*To believe in something
not yet proved and to underwrite it
with our lives; it is the only way
we can leave the future open.*

–Lillian Smith

❧

*Get off the sidewalk.
Walk the street with us into history.*

–Dolores Huerta

Be courageous.
It's one of the only places
left uncrowded.

—Anita Roddick

And the trouble is,
if you don't risk anything, you risk even more.

–Erica Jong

❧

You gain strength, courage
and confidence by every experience in which you
really stop to look fear in the face. You must do the
thing you think you cannot do.

–Eleanor Roosevelt

❧

I was always looking outside myself
for strength and confidence, but it comes from
within. It is there all the time.

–Anna Freud

UNCOMMON VOICES FROM UNCOMMON WOMEN™

Security is mostly a superstition.
It does not exist in nature. Life is either a
daring adventure or nothing.

–Helen Keller

❧

My favorite thing is to go where I've never been.

–Diane Arbus

❧

You cannot advance
when you concentrate on retreat.

–Sue Sikking

BRILLIANCE

*It is not easy to be a pioneer—
but oh, it is fascinating! I would not trade one
moment, even the worst moment,
for all the riches in the world.*

–Elizabeth Blackwell

❧

*Courage is the price
that Life exacts for granting peace.*

–Amelia Earhart

*The essential
conditions of everything
you do must be choice,
love, passion.*

–Nadia Boulanger

Find the passion.
It takes great passion and great energy
to do anything creative. I would go so far as to say
you can't do it without that passion.

–Agnes DeMille

❧

Passion is not
necessarily something we have,
it's something we choose.

–Susan Carlson

BRILLIANCE

*Life loves
to be taken by the lapel and told,
"I'm with you kid. Let's go."*

–Maya Angelou

❧

*One can never
consent to creep when one feels an
impulse to soar.*

–Helen Keller

❧

Talent is a flame. Genius is a fire.

–B. Williams

UNCOMMON VOICES FROM UNCOMMON WOMEN™

21

When in doubt, make a fool of yourself.
There is a microscopically thin line between
being brilliantly creative and acting like
the most gigantic idiot on earth.
So what the hell, leap!

–Cynthia Heimel

❧

Choose life!
Only that and always! At whatever risk.
To let life leak out, to let it wear away by the mere
passage of time, to withold giving and
spending it. . .is to choose nothing.

–Sister Helen Kelly

*When the world laughs at you, laugh back.
It's just as funny as you are.*

—Thomasina Horton

❧

*I'm the foe of moderation,
the champion of excess. I'd rather be
strongly wrong than weakly right.*

—Tallulah Bankhead

❧

*It's better to be a lion
for a day than a sheep all your life.*

—Sister Elizabeth Kenny

For the sake
of making a living we forget to live.

–Margaret Fuller

❧

Life is too short to short yourself on life.

–Terri Zadra

❧

That's our function
in life–to make a declarative statement.

–Corinne Jacker

UNCOMMON VOICES FROM UNCOMMON WOMEN™

24

If you are not
afraid to die, why be afraid to live?

–Joanna Sparks

❧

Life is in the here and now,
not in the there and afterwards.
This day, with all the travail and joy that
it brings to our doorstep, is the expression
of eternal life. Either we meet it,
we live it–or we miss it.

–Vimala Thakar

Earth is crammed with heaven.

–Elizabeth Barrett Browning

❧

*I don't want to get
to the end of my life and find that I just lived
the length of it. I want to have lived
the width of it as well.*

–Diane Ackerman

❧

Adventure is worthwhile in itself.

–Amelia Earhart

*Cherish forever
what makes you unique,
'cuz you're really a
yawn if it goes!*

–Bette Midler

*Why compare
yourself with others?
No one in the entire world can
do a better job of being
you than you.*

–Susan Carlson

❧

*Never compromise yourself.
You are all you've got.*

–Betty Ford

UNCOMMON VOICES FROM UNCOMMON WOMEN™

*He who walks
in another's tracks leaves no footprints.*

–Helen Ottway

❧

*You are unique,
and if that is not fulfilled, then something
has been lost.*

–Martha Graham

❧

*We relish news of our heroes,
forgetting that we are extraordinary
to somebody too.*

–Helen Hayes

BRILLIANCE

*Self-respect has nothing to do
with reputation or the approval of others.*

—Joan Didion

❧

*It's nice to be included
in people's fantasies, but you also like to be
accepted for your own sake.*

—Marilyn Monroe

❧

*Some of the most important things
in life aren't things.*

—Linda Ellerbee

*It's easy to be independent
when you've got money. But to be independent
when you haven't got a thing–
that's the Lord's test.*

–Mahalia Jackson

*I'll keep my personal dignity
and pride to the very end. It's a possession that
only I myself can part with.*

–Daisy Bates

*The best and most
beautiful things in the world cannot
be seen or even touched. They must be
felt with the heart.*

–Helen Keller

❧

*I would rather
have roses on my table than
diamonds on my neck.*

–Emma Goldman

BRILLIANCE

The more you get,
the more you got to take care of.

—Alice Dormann

❧

It's amazing how many
cares one loses when one decides not to be
something, but to be someone.

—Coco Chanel

❧

Until you've lost your
reputation, you never realize what a burden
it was or what freedom really is.

—Margaret Mitchell

Don't confuse fame with success.
Madonna is one; Helen Keller is the other.

−Erma Bombeck

❧

I've begun to think of myself
as 'independently wealthy' because I realize that
I carry within myself most of what I need
to make me happy.

−Cathleen Roundtree

❧

How we spend our days is,
of course, how we spend our lives.

−Annie Dillard

*When you get
into a tight place and it
seems that you can't go on,
hold on—for that's just the place
and the time that the
tide will turn.*

–Harriet Beecher Stowe

Life is not easy for any of us.
Early on in life I decided that I would not be
vanquished and that I would remain cheerful in
the face of circumstances.

–Rose Kennedy

❧

You can't be brave
if you've only had wonderful things
happen to you.

–Mary Tyler Moore

You have to have faith
that there is a reason you go through
certain things. I can't say I am glad to go through
pain, but in a way one must, in order to gain
courage and really feel joy.

–Carol Burnett

❧

One thing I learned the hard way
was that it doesn't pay to get discouraged.
Keeping busy and making optimism a way of life
can restore your faith in yourself.

–Lucille Ball

*There are two ways of
meeting difficulties. You can alter the difficulties,
or you can alter yourself meeting them.*

—Phyllis Bottome

❧

*No life is so hard that you can't make
it easier by the way you take it.*

—Ellen Glasgow

❧

*The way I see it,
if you want the rainbow, you gotta
put up with the rain.*

—Dolly Parton

BRILLIANCE

*Laughter in the face of reality
is probably the finest sound there is. In fact,
a good time to laugh is any time you can.*

–Linda Ellerbee

❧

*Experience is pure gold.
Experience is what you get when you don't get
what you want.*

Ann Landers

❧

*I thank God for my handicaps,
for through them I have found myself,
my work and my God.*

–Helen Keller

*Having it all doesn't
necessarily mean having it all at once.*

–Stephanie Luetkehaus

❧

The force of the waves is in their perseverance.

–Gila Guri

❧

*You may have
to fight a battle more than once to win it.*

–Margaret Thatcher

BRILLIANCE

Be patient.
Our prayers are always answered,
but not always on the exact day
we'd like them to be.

–Marjorie Turner

❧

Comedy is tragedy plus time.

–Carrol Burnett

❧

Just pray for a tough hide
and a tender heart.

–Ruth Graham

God doesn't give breaks.
He gives breakthroughs.

–June Martin

❧

I know God will not give me
anything I can't handle. I just wish that
He didn't trust me so much.

–Mother Teresa

❧

I make the most
of all that comes and the least
of all that goes.

–Sara Teasdale

I don't look at what I've lost.
I look instead at what I have left.

–Betty Ford

❧

So much has been given to me;
I have no time to ponder over that which
has been denied.

–Helen Keller

❧

Just don't give up trying to do
what you really want to do. Where there is
love and inspiration, I don't think
you can go wrong.

–Ella Fitzgerald

UNCOMMON VOICES FROM UNCOMMON WOMEN™

Success
doesn't come to you.
You go to it.

–Marva Collins

Anyone who says
the days of opportunity are over is copping out.

–Ann Landers

Winners have the ability
to adapt to the terrain. They take responsibility
for their own career path.

–Mary Cunningham

It is more important to know
where you are going than to get there quickly.
Never mistake activity for achievement.

–Mabel Newcomber

UNCOMMON VOICES FROM UNCOMMON WOMEN™

*The first duty of a human being is to find
your real job and do it.*

–Charlotte Perkins Gilman

❧

*No one can arrive
from being talented alone. God gives talent;
work transforms talent into genius.*

–Anna Pavlova

❧

*I don't wait for moods.
You accomplish nothing if you do that. Your mind
must know it has got to get down to earth.*

–Pearl S. Buck

BRILLIANCE

Some people regard discipline
as a chore. For me, it's a kind of order
that sets me free to fly.

–Julie Andrews

❧

My success was not based so much on any
great intelligence but on great common sense.

–Helen Gurley Brown

❧

Champions take responsibility.
When the ball comes over the net, you can
be sure I want the ball.

–Billie Jean King

The person who knows
'how' will always have a job. The person who
knows 'why' will always be his boss.

–Diane Ravitch

❧

Be prepared.
It's better to have it and not need it, than to
need it and not have it.

–Elizabeth Ann Nolan

❧

The formula for success is simple:
Do your best and someone might like it.

–Marva Collins

*Doing your best
at this moment puts you in the best place
for the next moment.*

–Oprah Winfrey

❧

*When we do the best we can,
we never know what miracle is wrought in our life,
or in the life of another.*

–Helen Keller

*It's amazing how lucky
I become whenever I consistently put out
my best effort.*

—Cybil Franklin

&

*Luck means the hardships
you have not hesitated to endure;
the long nights you have devoted to your work.
Luck means the appointments you have never
failed to keep, the airplanes you
never failed to catch.*

—Margaret Clement

BRILLIANCE

I was born to shiver
in the draft from an open mind.

−Phyllis McGinley

❧

Innovators are inevitably controversial.

−Eva Le Gallienne

❧

Creative minds
have always been known to survive
any kind of bad training.

−Anna Freud

*It's a mistake to
surround yourself only with
people just like you. Throw off that worn
comforter–and replace it with a crazy quilt of
different and imaginative people.
Then watch the ideas erupt!*

–Betty Bender

*Imagination
is the highest kite you can fly.*

–Lauren Bacall

Excellence makes people nervous.

–Shana Alexander

❧

*No man or woman who tries
to pursue an ideal in his or her own way
is without enemies.*

Daisy Bates

❧

*If I'm too strong
for some people, that's their problem.*

–Glenda Jackson

*Being powerful is like being a lady.
If you have to tell people you are, you aren't.*

–Margaret Thatcher

*The key to whatever success I enjoy
today is: Don't ask. Do.*

–Vikki Carr

*Self-reliance is the answer
to the question, "Who can I turn to?"*

–Patricia Sampson

*It's amazing
how fast doors open to us when we dare
to take control of a situation.*

–Catherine Ponder

Doubt who you will, but never yourself.

–Christine Bovee

*Instead of this absurd division
into sexes they ought to class people
as static and dynamic.*

*If at first you don't succeed,
you're probably lucky.*

—Margaret L. Clement

❧

*The fame you earn
has a different taste from the fame
that is forced upon you.*

—Gloria Vanderbilt

❧

*I climbed the ladder
of success wrong by wrong.*

—Pat Brooks

BRILLIANCE

*Mistakes are a part
of the dues one pays for a full life.*

–Sophia Loren

෪

*Show me a person
who has never made a mistake and I'll show you
somebody who has never achieved much.*

–Joan Collins

෪

*We ought to be able to learn some
things second-hand. There is not enough time for
us to make all the mistakes ourselves.*

–Harriet Hall

UNCOMMON VOICES FROM UNCOMMON WOMEN™

57

*A mistake
is simply another way of doing things.*

–Katharine Graham

*I'll match my flops with anybody's
but I wouldn't have missed them. Flops are a part
of life's menu and I've never been one
to miss out on any of the courses.*

–Rosalind Russell

*There are people
who take the heart out of you,
and there are people
who put it back.*

–Elizabeth David

*Those who are lifting
the world upward and onward are those who
encourage more than criticize.*

–Elizabeth Harrison

&

*The best index
to a person's character is how he
treats people who can't do him any good–
and how he treats people who
can't fight back.*

–Abigail Van Buren

*Appreciation in any form
at any time brightens anyone's existence.*

–Ruth Stafford Peale

❧

*Sandwich every bit
of criticism between two layers of praise.*

–Mary Kay Ash

❧

*Listening, not imitation,
is the sincerest form of flattery.*

–Joyce Brothers

*As novices, we think
we're entirely responsible for the way
people treat us. I have long since learned
that we are responsible only for the
way we treat people.*

—Rose Lane

❧

*Expect people
to be better than they are;
it helps them to become better. But don't
be disappointed when they are not;
it helps them to keep trying.*

—Merry Browne

*Ideas are a dime a dozen,
but the men and women who implement them
are priceless.*

–Mary Kay Ash

❧

*If you have a company,
hire children to sit on your board. Then listen
and learn. Their instincts are excellent.
They cherish lived-up-to promises
and real guarantees.*

–Faith Popcorn

*You cannot manage
men into battle. You manage things;
you lead people.*

–Admiral Grace Murray Hopper

*Never doubt
that a small group of thoughtful,
committed people can change the world.
Indeed, it is the only thing
that ever has.*

–Margaret Mead

*I don't think you should
ever manage something that you don't
care passionately about.*

–Deborah Coleman

❧

*I keep an eye on the bottomline,
but it's not an overriding obsession. To me,
P and L doesn't just mean "profit and loss"–
it also means "people and love."*

–Mary Kay Ash

65

*What matters today is
not the difference between those who believe
and those who do not believe, but the
difference between those who care
and those who don't.*

–Abbe Pire

❧

*If the future is to remain
open and free, we need people who can tolerate
the unknown, who will not need the support of
completely worked-out systems or
traditional blueprints
from the past.*

–Margaret Mead

BRILLIANCE

*Everybody wants
to do something to help, but nobody
wants to be first.*

—Pearl Bailey

❧

*Concern should drive us
into action and not into a depression.*

—Karen Horney

❧

*Those who think
they have no responsibilities are those
who have not sought them out.*

—Mary Lyon

UNCOMMON VOICES FROM UNCOMMON WOMEN™

67

*You have not lived
a perfect day, even though you have earned
your money, unless you have done something
for someone who will never
be able to repay you.*

–Ruth Smeltzer

❧

*The only thing
that makes one place more attractive
to me than another is the quantity
of heart I find in it.*

–Jane Welsh Carlyle

*The history of every country begins in
the heart of a man or a woman.*

–Willa Cather

❧

*This I know. This I believe with all my heart.
If we want a free and peaceful world, if we want to
make deserts bloom and man to grow to greater
dignity as a human being–we can do it!*

–Eleanor Roosevelt

❧

*These are the hard times in which
a genius would wish to live. Great necessities call
forth great leaders.*

–Abigail Adams

UNCOMMON VOICES FROM UNCOMMON WOMEN™

*After the verb
'To Love'... 'To Help'
is the most beautiful
verb in the world.*

—Bertha von Suttner

BRILLIANCE

*What the world
really needs is more love
and less paper work.*

–Pearl Bailey

❧

*The human heart,
at whatever age, opens to the heart
that opens in return.*

–Marie Edgeworth

❧

*If you have knowledge,
let others light their candles at it.*

–Margaret Fuller

*The fragrance always
stays in the hand that gives the rose.*

–Hada Bejar

❦

*Blessed are those
who can give without remembering
and take without forgetting.*

–Elizabeth Bibesco

UNCOMMON VOICES FROM UNCOMMON WOMEN™

72

BRILLIANCE

The heart that gives–gathers.

–Hannah Moore

❧

*To give without any reward,
or any notice, has a special quality of its own.*

–Anne Morrow Lindbergh

❧

*'Twas her thinking
of others made you think of her.*

–Elizabeth Barrett Browning

BRILLIANCE

*Empathy is
your pain I feel in my heart.*

–Hospice Volunteer

❧

*Since when do you have
to agree with people to defend
them from injustice?*

–Lillian Hellman

❧

*The greatest achievements are those
that benefit others.*

–Lillian Gilcrest

*We must have places
where children can have a whole group
of adults they can trust.*

–Margaret Mead

❧

*I think leaders should
encourage the next generation not just
to follow, but to overtake.*

–Anita Roddick

❧

Light tomorrow with today.

–Elizabeth Barrett Browning

Never mistake knowledge for wisdom. One helps you make a living; the other helps you make a life.

—Sandra Carey

BRILLIANCE

*I have learned a philosophy
in the great University of Hard Knocks.
I have learned to live each day as it comes, and not
to borrow trouble by dreading tomorrow.*

–Dorothy Dix

❧

*If only we'd stop trying to be happy,
we could have a pretty good time.*

–Edith Wharton

❧

Worry is a misuse of the imagination.

–Audrey Woodhall

*If something is wrong, fix it
if you can. But train yourself not to worry.
Worry never fixes anything.*

–Mary Hemingway

❧

*Advice is what we
ask for when we already know the answer
but wish we didn't.*

–Erica Jong

❧

*The best advice
yet given is that you don't have to take it.*

–Libbie Fudim

*Think wrongly, if you please,
but in all cases think for yourself.*

–Doris Lessing

❧

*You can never get yourself
or anybody else into trouble by being honest.*

–Rose Lane

❧

*My dog and cat
have taught me a great lesson
in life…shed a lot.*

–Susan Carlson

UNCOMMON VOICES FROM UNCOMMON WOMEN™

BRILLIANCE

*One loses so many
laughs by not laughing at oneself.*

–Sara Jeannette Duncan

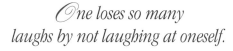

*There is always something
left to love. And if you ain't learned that,
you ain't learned nothing.*

–Lorraine Hansberry

*You grow up the day
you have your first real laugh–at yourself.*

–Ethel Barrymore

*God always has
another custard pie up his sleeve.*

—Lynn Redgrave

❧

*Believe there is a great power
silently working all things for good, behave
yourself and never mind the rest.*

—Beatrix Potter

❧

*Never let the urgent
crowd out the important.*

—Kelly Catlin Walker.

*The main thing
is to keep the main thing
the main thing.*

–Kelly Ann Rothaus

❧

*Time is a very precious gift
from God; so precious that it is only
given to us moment by moment.*

–Amelia Barr

❧

For fast-acting relief try slowing down.

–Lily Tomlin

*I believe there are more
urgent and honorable occupations than
the incomparable waste of time
we call suffering.*

–Colette

*Never face facts;
if you do you'll never get up in the morning.*

–Marlo Thomas

*When you make a mountain
out of a molehill, you have to climb it.*

–Sue Sikking

❧

*The perception of a problem
is always relative. Your headache feels terrific
to the druggist.*

–Ramona E. F. Arnett

❧

*As important as 'hanging on'
is knowing when to 'let go.'*

–Sherri DeWitt

*If you obey
all the rules you miss
all the fun.*

–Katharine Hepburn

*A little of what
you fancy does you good.*

–Marie Lloyd

*Here's a rule I recommend.
Never practice two vices at once.*

–Tallulah Bankhead

*Between two evils,
I always pick the one I never tried before.*

–Mae West

Too much of a good thing is wonderful.

—Mae West

*I generally avoid
temptation unless I can't resist it.*

—Mae West

To err is human—but it feels divine.

—Mae West

*If you always do
what interests you, then at least
one person is pleased.*

–Katharine Hepburn

*Happiness is something
that comes into our lives through doors we
don't even remember leaving open.*

–Rose Lane

*Joy seems to me a step
beyond happiness. Happiness is a sort of
atmosphere you can live in sometimes when you're
lucky. Joy is a light that fills you with hope
and faith and love.*

–Adela Rogers St. Johns

❧

*You will do foolish things,
but do them with enthusiasm.*

–Colette

Love doesn't
make the world go 'round.
Love is what makes the
ride worthwhile.

—Audrey Woodhall

I think we're here for each other.

–Carol Burnett

❧

You can't be human alone.

–Margaret Kuhn

❧

*I want to love first,
and live incidentally.*

–Zelda Fitzgerald

There is time for work.
And time for love. That leaves no other time.

—Coco Chanel

❧

When you love someone,
all your saved-up wishes start coming out.

—Elizabeth Bowen

❧

Love is a game that two can play
and both can win.

—Eva Gabor

Love is like fresh bread.
It has to be re-made all the time, made new.

–Ursula K. LeGuin

❧

Familiarity,
truly cultivated, can breed love.

–Dr. Joyce Brothers

❧

If you love someone,
then hurry up and show it.

–Rose Zadra, age 6

*Expressed affection is
the best of all methods to use when
you want to light a glow in someone's
heart and to feel it in your own.*

–Ruth Stafford Peale

❧

*One of the oldest human needs
is having someone wonder where you are when
you don't come home at night.*

–Margaret Mead

*The motto
should not be, "Forgive one another."
Rather, "Understand one another."*

–Emma Goldman

❧

Never go to bed mad. Stay up and fight.

–Phyllis Diller

❧

*Trouble is a part of life,
and if you don't share it, you don't give
the person who loves you a chance
to love you enough.*

–Dinah Shore

Go ahead and cry. I'll catch your tears.

–Jileen Russell

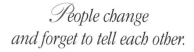

*People change
and forget to tell each other.*

–Lillian Hellman

*If you haven't forgiven yourself
something, how can you forgive others?*

–Dolores Huerta

BRILLIANCE

We lose a lot of time hating people.

—Marian Anderson

❧

You cannot
shake hands with a clenched fist.

—Golda Meir

❧

Love your enemies—it will
drive them nuts.

—Eleanor Doan

BRILLIANCE

Love people.
Use things. Not vice-versa.

–Kelly Ann Rothaus

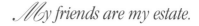

My friends are my estate.

–Emily Dickinson

It's the friends you can
call up at 4 A.M. that matter.

–Marlene Dietrich

*You never know
when you're making a memory.*

–Rickie Lee Jones

❧

*Lots of people want
to ride with you in the limo,
but what you want is someone who will take
the bus with you when the
limo breaks down.*

–Oprah Winfrey

❧

You are loved. If so, what else matters?

–Edna St. Vincent Millay

UNCOMMON VOICES FROM UNCOMMON WOMEN™

*Turn around and
you're two, turn around and
you're four, turn around and
you're a young girl going
out of my door.*

—Malvina Reynolds, "Turn Around," 1958

We mothered this nation.
*And we have no intention of abandoning our
roles as nurturer or wife, mother, loving daughter,
tax-paying citizen, homemaker, breadwinner.*

—Liz Carpenter

❦

*Motherhood is still the biggest gamble
in the world. It is the glorious life force.
It's huge and scary—it's an act of
infinite optimism.*

—Gilda Radner

Making the decision to have a child–
it's momentous. It is to decide forever to have your
heart go walking around outside your body.

—Elizabeth Stone

❧

I saw pure love when my son
looked at me, and I knew that I had to make
a good life for the two of us.

—Suzanne Somers

❧

At work you think of the children at home.
At home you think of the work you've left undone.
The struggle within yourself tears at the heart.

—Golda Meir

BRILLIANCE

A mother is a person who, seeing there are only four pieces of pie for five people, promptly announces she never did care for pie.

—Tenneva Jordan

❧

We didn't have much but we sure had plenty.

—Sherry Thomas

❧

The walks and talks we have with our two-year-olds in red boots have a great deal to do with the values they will cherish as adults.

—Edith F. Hunter

UNCOMMON VOICES FROM UNCOMMON WOMEN™

*The real menace in dealing with a
five-year-old is that in no time at all you begin
to sound like a five-year-old.*

—Jean Kerr

*To grown people a girl of fifteen is a
child still; to herself she is very old and very real;
more real, perhaps, than ever before or after.*

—Margaret Widdemer

*You have to love your children unselfishly.
That's hard, but it's the only way.*

—Barbara Bush

*Parents learn a lot from
their children about coping with life.*

—Muriel Spark

❧

*There's a lot more to being a woman than
being a mother, but there's one hell of a lot more
to being a mother than most people suspect.*

—Roseanne Barr

❧

*I learned so much more about
men by having a son.*

—Barbra Streisand

*We want our children to fit in and to stand out.
We rarely address the conflict between these goals.*

—Ellen Goodman

❧

*The elders still say: "You know I have been young,
but you can never have been old." But today's kids
can reply: "You've never been young in the world
I am young in, and you never can be."*

—Margaret Mead

❧

*We had a disappointing experience with
our children—they all grew up.*

—Leslie Bonaventure

*No matter how old a mother is
she watches her middle-aged children
for signs of improvement.*

—Florida Scott-Maxwell

*Your children are always your babies,
even if they have gray hair.*

—Janet Leigh

*Choose to have a career early
and a family late. Or choose to have a family
early and a career late—but plan a long life.*

—Dr. Janet Rowley

It is
never too late
to be what you might
have been.

—George Eliot

BRILLIANCE

*Life is a process of becoming,
a combination of states we have to go through.
Where people fail is that they wish to elect
a state and remain in it.*

–Anais Nin

❧

*You may have a fresh start
any moment you choose, for this thing
that we call "failure" is not the falling down,
but the staying down.*

–Mary Pickford

BRILLIANCE

*You should always
know when you're shifting gears in life.
You should leave your era; it should
never leave you.*

—Leontyne Price

❧

*The final forming of a person's
character lies in their own hands.*

—Anne Frank

UNCOMMON VOICES FROM UNCOMMON WOMEN™

BRILLIANCE

*When I was growing up
I always wanted to be someone. Now I realize
I should have been more specific.*

–Lily Tomlin

❧

*The trouble with life is,
you're half way through it before you realize
it's a 'do it yourself' thing.*

–Annie Zadra

*Every human being
on this earth is born with the tragedy
that he has to grow up. A lot of people
don't have the courage to do it.*

–Helen Hayes

*I think somehow
we learn who we really are and then live
with that decision.*

–Eleanor Roosevelt

*Do you know why grown-ups
are always asking little kids what they want
to be when they grow up? It's because
they're looking for ideas.*

–Paula Poundstone

*Life is what happens to you
when you are making other plans.*

–Betty Talmadge

BRILLIANCE

*In the long run, we shape our lives
and we shape ourselves. The process never ends
until we die. And the choices we make are
ultimately our responsibility.*

–Eleanor Roosevelt

❧

*You can have the results
you say you want, or you can have all the reasons
why you can't have them. But you can't
have both. Reasons or results.
You get to choose.*

–Susan Carlson

*Adventure is something you seek
for pleasure, or even profit, like a gold rush;
but experience is what really happens to you in the
long run—the truth that finally overtakes you.*

–Katherine Anne Porter

❧

*If the future road
looks ominous or unpromising,
and the roads back uninviting, then we need to
gather our resolve and, carrying only
the necessary baggage, step off that
road into another direction.*

–Maya Angelou

*Age is
not important
unless you're
a cheese.*

—Helen Hayes

I am not a has-been. I'm a will be.

–Lauren Bacall

❧

Sooner or later
I'm going to die, but I'm not going to retire.

–Margaret Mead

❧

We turn not older
with years, but newer every day.

–Emily Dickinson

I believe in hard work.
It keeps the wrinkles out of the mind and the spirit.
It helps to keep a woman going.

–Helena Rubenstein

In a word, I am always busy,
which is perhaps the chief reason why
I am always well.

–Elizabeth Cady Stanton

*You never grow old
until you've lost all your marvels.*

–Merry Browne

❧

*The older I grow, the more
I listen to people who don't say much.*

–Germain Glidden

❧

I shall not grow conservative with age.

–Elizabeth Cady Stanton

*Life is the first gift;
love is the second; and understanding
is the third.*

—Marge Piercy

*I look forward
to growing old and wise
and audacious.*

—Glenda Jackson

BRILLIANCE

If you rest, you rust.

–Helen Hayes

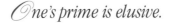

*Regret is an appalling
waste of energy. You can't build on it;
it's only good for wallowing in.*

Katherine Mansfield

One's prime is elusive.

–Muriel Spark

BRILLIANCE

I have no regrets.
I wouldn't have lived my life the way I did
if I was going to worry about what
people were going to say.

—Ingrid Bergman

❧

What a lovely surprise
to discover how unlonely being
alone can be.

—Ellen Burstyn

UNCOMMON VOICES FROM UNCOMMON WOMEN™

122

*You can take no credit
for beauty at sixteen. But if you
are beautiful at sixty, it will be
your soul's own doing.*

–Marie Stopes

❧

*You know, of course,
that it is never too late to begin.
Why, Grandma Moses didn't start
her painting career until she
was seventy-six!*

–Carrie Bethard

Beauty is not caused. It is.

—Emily Dickinson

*I love my past.
I love my present. I'm not ashamed
of what I've had, and I'm not sad because
I have it no longer.*

—Colette

We are always the same age inside.

—Gertrude Stein

❧

If I had my life to live over,
I'd like to make more mistakes next time.
I would climb more mountains and swim more
rivers. I would eat more ice cream and less beans.
I would perhaps have more actual troubles,
but fewer imaginary ones.

—Nadine Stair, age 81

UNCOMMON VOICES FROM UNCOMMON WOMEN™

125

BRILLIANCE

It seems to me
we can never give up longing
and wishing while we are alive. There are
certain things we feel to be beautiful and good,
and we must hunger for them.

–George Eliot

❧

What a wonderful life I've had.
I only wish I'd realized it sooner.

–Colette

UNCOMMON VOICES FROM UNCOMMON WOMEN™

126

*The world
is round and the place
which may seem like the end,
may also be only
the beginning.*

—Ivy Baker Priest

Also available from Compendium Publishing are these spirited
and compelling companion books of great quotations.

Because of You™
Celebrating the Difference You Make™

Forever Remembered™
A Gift for the Grieving Heart™

I Believe in You™
To your heart, your dream and the difference you make.

Little Miracles™
To renew your dreams, lift your spirits, and strengthen your resolve.™

Reach for the Stars™
Give up the Good to Go for the Great.™

Thank You™
In appreciation of you, and all that you do.™

Together We Can™
Celebrating the Power of a Team and a Dream.™

To Your Success™
Thoughts to Give Wings to Your Work and Your Dreams™

Whatever It Takes™
A Journey into the Heart of Human Achievement™

You've Got a Friend™
Thoughts to Celebrate the Joy of Friendship™

These books may be ordered directly from the publisher (800) 914-3327.
But please try your bookstore first!

www.compendiuminc.com